Manuel Irman

The London Underground Railway

An Attempt to Solve the Nineteenth Century's Urban Traffic Problems and the Present Time Consequences

GRIN Verlag

Bibliografische Information der Deutschen Nationalbibliothek:

Die Deutsche Bibliothek verzeichnet diese Publikation in der Deutschen National-
bibliografie; detaillierte bibliografische Daten sind im Internet über http://dnb.d-
nb.de/ abrufbar.

Dieses Werk sowie alle darin enthaltenen einzelnen Beiträge und Abbildungen
sind urheberrechtlich geschützt. Jede Verwertung, die nicht ausdrücklich vom
Urheberrechtsschutz zugelassen ist, bedarf der vorherigen Zustimmung des Verla-
ges. Das gilt insbesondere für Vervielfältigungen, Bearbeitungen, Übersetzungen,
Mikroverfilmungen, Auswertungen durch Datenbanken und für die Einspeicherung
und Verarbeitung in elektronische Systeme. Alle Rechte, auch die des auszugsweisen
Nachdrucks, der fotomechanischen Wiedergabe (einschließlich Mikrokopie) sowie
der Auswertung durch Datenbanken oder ähnliche Einrichtungen, vorbehalten.

Impressum:

Copyright © 2006 GRIN Verlag GmbH
Druck und Bindung: Books on Demand GmbH, Norderstedt Germany
ISBN: 978-3-656-15801-1

GRIN - Your knowledge has value

Der GRIN Verlag publiziert seit 1998 wissenschaftliche Arbeiten von Studenten, Hochschullehrern und anderen Akademikern als eBook und gedrucktes Buch. Die Verlagswebsite www.grin.com ist die ideale Plattform zur Veröffentlichung von Hausarbeiten, Abschlussarbeiten, wissenschaftlichen Aufsätzen, Dissertationen und Fachbüchern.

Besuchen Sie uns im Internet:

http://www.grin.com/

http://www.facebook.com/grincom

http://www.twitter.com/grin_com

The London Underground Railway

An Attempt to Solve the Nineteenth Century's Urban
Traffic Problems and the Present Time Consequences

Maturaarbeit 2006

TSME Frauenfeld

Author: Manuel Irman

Submission Date: 28th January 2006

Subject: English

Preface

Walking or travelling by public traffic is the easiest way of moving inside large cities. That is what I have experienced as a tourist on several trips. Ever since, I have been fascinated by the easiness of travelling through cities by public transport compared to exhausting car trips and hours of congestion. It even seemed safer and more comfortable to me and so I became interested in the means of transport provided to the public by cities. Underground railways attracted me in particular as they are widely unknown in Switzerland. The one I have used most is the *London Underground* and it has given me many opportunities to study its characteristics and whilst doing so many questions appeared in mind.

This work gives me a unique opportunity to disclose some of the secrets and to display them in a historical context. As the topic's field of investigation is quite large, some explicit questions are asked in the introductory chapter. In order to answer them, I mainly focused on local circumstances and tried to connect them with the *Tube*. Of course, for the development of the City of London there is more at stake than just local history. So to take this into consideration, I first rolled up the process of how London had been developed in relation to national or European circumstances. At last, the first underground railway line was under construction when England reached its peak of power. This must have been a specific answer to the very situation of traffic in London at the period as well as to its prior development. But how did it all take place? This paper is providing some answers.

Manuel Irman

Contents

1 Introduction

London was the first city in the world to start building underground railway lines. In 1863, the first line from Paddington Station to Farringdon Street was opened.[1] It took more than three decades until the first town in continental Europe (Budapest, opened in 1896) also decided to build a railway underground.[2] The construction of London's Underground was therefore remarkably early, which leads to the following question: *What circumstances led to choose this form of public traffic at this point of time?* Two chapters are dedicated to London's history; once in a general sense, and then more specifically applied to the development of traffic and transportation before the 19th century. The following chapters show the progress of public traffic from 1800 to the opening of railway lines and the steps needed in order to realise an underground railway system. Finally, the present situation at the beginning of the 21st century is of interest and the question, *whether the Underground had been the right choice* – even for these days. This paper considers political, social, and technical … in order to answer the following issue: *What circumstance(s) and reason(s) played a role in taking the decision to construct a railway line below and why this early?* Furthermore, a second issue is to be answered: *What are the consequences for London by the early 21st century, having a railway system that is aged more than 140 years and what influence did the Underground have on London's development from then to now?*

2 London's Urban Development in History

The site where the modern City of London was established must have been important to the people many centuries before. This chapter investigates briefly on how London grew from a countryside settlement to a metropolitan city. Detailed traffic issues in this context will be dealt with further below.

2.1 Important Settlement

Before the Romans came to Britain and founded *Londinium* in the year of 43 AD, the place is supposed to have been a rural area. Although some pre-Roman finds have been made, it is most likely that they only show the importance of the site but not the existence of a larger settlement.[3] Londinium was thought to be a permanent military camp for Roman legions but

---

[1] BARKER, T.C./ROBBINS, Michael: *A History of London Transport, Vol. 1*, London 1963, p. 99.
[2] LOXTON, Howard: Railways, London et al. 1968, p. 139.
[3] WIKIPEDIA: *History of London*.

their principle centre was in modern Colchester. Seventeen years later, after a failed uprising of the local tribe of the Iceni, Londinium burned to the ground. The Romans rebuilt their damaged camp and it became the capital of *Britannia*.[4]

By 410 AD, the Romans had abandoned Londinium and their occupation and their occupation came to an end.[5] After a quiet era of nearly two hundred years settlement was revived by Saxon invaders. The new city was named *Lundenwic* and meant *London Port*. During the late Saxon leadership Lundenwic became known as *Lundenburgh* when the focus of settlement turned from the old port back to the old city.[6]

2.2 Mediaeval Town

After a short period of Danish reign, the Normans invaded Britain in 1066 and the Saxon era came to an end.[7] Consequently, the town of Westminster which was only a short bit upstream London became the royal capital of England. William Rufus, the son of William the Conqueror, who had led the Norman invasion, started constructing Westminster Hall, which became the main royal residence throughout the entire Middle Ages.[8] By the year of 1300, London's population had reached the considerable number of one hundred thousand citizens.[9] In 1348, the continent-wide bubonic plague reached England and every second Londoner was killed in effect.[10]

The area between Westminster and London was completely urbanised by the year of 1600, when population reached a size of more than 200,000 people. During the mediaeval epoch, several royal families ruled England and the City of London prospered due to increasing mercantilism. In spite of this, the city's sanitation was horrible and the bubonic plague broke out sixteen times between 1348 and 1666. The buildings were mostly made of wood and the threat of fire was omnipresent.[11] The streets were narrow and twisty[12] as it is still recognisable in other mediaeval European towns.

---

[4] THE OFFICIAL WEBSITE FOR LONDON: *City Guide*.
[5] IBID.
[6] WIKIPEDIA: *History of London*.
[7] THE OFFICIAL WEBSITE FOR LONDON: *City Guide*.
[8] WIKIPEDIA: *History of London*.
[9] IBID.
[10] THE OFFICIAL WEBSITE FOR LONDON: *City Guide*.
[11] WIKIPEDIA: *History of London*.
[12] IBID.

2.3 The Great Fire

On the morning of 2 September 1666, not even a year after the last plague had killed a sixth of London's population, a fire broke out in the royal bakery in Pudding Lane. The fire spread rapidly and destroyed one wooden house after another, benefiting from the heat of the previous summer which had dried the roofs well. Five days later *The Great Fire* was under control but eighty percent of the city had been destroyed and about 80,000 people were homeless. After this incident, the mediaeval part of the City of London was wiped out.[13]

Soon after the city was struck by the huge fire, planners designed a new town with wide and representative roads. Unfortunately, the house proprietors rejected such plans and were not willing to give up their properties. Eventually, the verdict was to rebuild London almost as it had looked before. Although buildings were now made of stone instead of wood, the remained tiny and narrow.[14]

2.4 Modern Times

Up to the beginning of the 19th century, London grew rapidly to a population of one million inhabitants, which was due to migration, mainly as a result of the flourishing trade. Most of the early immigrants came from all over the country seeking their luck in London only to be followed by continental European tradesmen.[15]

Shortly after 1500, London had become the largest town on the planet and held this status until 1925, when New York surpassed it.[16] Between the beginning and the end of the 19th century, the population had increased six-fold and this was not without effect on the city's street life. London increased dramatically in size and it became more and more urgent to find a solution to improve the traffic flow. A similar importance was given to usable sewers in order to avoid epidemics and improve air quality in this sometimes horribly stinky town.[17]

3 Increasing Traffic and an Unsuitable Network of Streets

The Fire of 1666 is often thought to be a sudden cut in the city's history and London to have received a completely different face. Obviously, this was not the case and it is therefore

---

[13] ALBIG, Jörg-Uwe: „Das geheime Leben der Kapitale", in: *Geo Epoche. Das Magazin für Geschichte 18 (London. Geschichte einer Weltstadt, 1558-1945)*, Hamburg 2005, p. 74ff.
[14] IBID., p. 76ff.
[15] BRITISH BROADCASTING CORPORATION (BBC): *Social History (b)*.
[16] MISCHER, Olaf/OTTO, Frank: „London. Stadtgeschichte" (Chronik), in: *Geo Epoche. Das Magazin für Geschichte 18 (London. Geschichte einer Weltstadt, 1558-1945)*, Hamburg 2005, p. 174ff.
[17] FRÖMEL, Susanne: „Moderne Zeiten", in: *Geo Epoche. Das Magazin für Geschichte 18 (London. Geschichte einer Weltstadt, 1558-1945)*, Hamburg 2005, p. 124ff.

important not only to study the situation after London had been rebuilt but also to consider the circumstances the city had to deal with before. This view is supported by Dr. John Schofield who said that "we have perhaps been overimpressed by the Great Fire, and [...] the Fire [...] devastated only about a third of conurbation of London then standing."[18] Many houses remained wooden and it took generations to change their appearance to a more modern one. But he also admits that the Fire created a certain opportunity to shape the city differently.[19]

Although the source used in chapter 2.3 suspects eighty percent of the buildings had burnt down, Schofield mentions only a number of about thirty percent. This leads to the conclusion that facts in this context have to be used carefully, but there is no doubt that the opportunity to improve the city significantly had been missed to a large extent.

3.1   17th Century Traffic Situation

3.1.1   Contemporary Accounts

By New Year's Day of 1660, Samuel Pepys, a higher public official, opened a diary – a remarkably unusual course of action in those days. The reason is rather unclear but it is a unique and valuable document which provides answers about social and public live in London during the decade that followed 1660. Pepys held the same (cold) distance in describing events no matter whether it was about garden flowers or a public hanging.[20]

According to Sir John Oldham, a contemporary of Pepys, the scene on London's roads was everything but orderly and comfortable. He was not able to sleep quietly due to bells, the poems of night watches, the noise of drunken people and, in the morning, the sound of all sorts of animals setting in.[21] Whatsoever, it was no better during daytime when Samuel Pepys was forced, in 1661, to remain in a hackney carriage for one and a half hours because the traffic congestion was so bad. Five days later, the traffic jams made him go shopping instead of continuing his journey (sic!).[22]

3.1.2   Public Transport

During the 17th century, London's population increased by about three hundred percent form around 200,000 to 600,000 inhabitants.[23] Such a growth of population (not the percent-

[18] BRITISH BROADCASTING CORPORATION (BBC): Social History (a).
[19] IBID.
[20] ALBIG, Jörg-Uwe: „Das geheime Leben der Kapitale", in: Geo Epoche. Das Magazin für Geschichte 18 (London. Geschichte einer Weltstadt, 1558-1945), Hamburg 2005, p. 62ff.
[21] IBID., p. 68.
[22] BRITISH BROADCASTING CORPORATION (BBC): Social History (b).
[23] WIKIPEDIA: History of London.

age but the number) had not been seen until then and according to chapter 2.2 the streets did not have the right capacity and were to become overcrowded within a short time. "Travel within the capital was also becoming more as we would recognise it today"[24], says Bruce Robinson and is pointing into the same direction.

Yet from 1625, hackney carriages were licensed and regulated by Parliament *(Hackney Coach Commission)* to run passenger services and at the same time *wherries* (a kind of river-buses) were transporting people on the river Thames.[25] The reason to licence the coaches was to prevent further congestions while the number of vehicles increased quickly in order to carry the growing number of citizens which occurred simultaneously. Nevertheless, a growing number of road-users were demanding for more means of public traffic and the number of permissions had to be raised by the authorities.[26] Eventually, a final solution to avoid the worst congestions was not only given by licensing the carriages because pedestrians were largely responsible for jamming the streets and they were not able to afford the high charges for public traffic until the later 19th century whatsoever.[27] In 1813, King George IV, being aware of this problem, gave order to his most favoured architect to enlarge streets and squares to a size cities like Paris already had.[28]

3.2 Attempts to Improve Streets to a Dignified Appearance

3.2.1 Failed Attempts

As we approach the early 19th century, however, there has to be mentioned that some work on the infrastructure had been done before the reign of King George IV. As explained in chapter 2.3, city planners of the post-Fire period were not successful in convincing London's house owners with their plans.

Christopher Wren, the architect of St. Paul's Cathedral after the Great Fire, proposed to build main access roads from all four directions into Central London and to enlarge the most public places into representative "piazzas".[29] He also thought of standardising the width of the streets into three categories which would have simplified further city planning enormously. With regard to these proposals, none of them had been taken over neither by the people of

---

[24] BRITISH BROADCASTING CORPORATION (BBC): *Social History (b)*.
[25] IBID.
[26] BARKER, T.C./ROBBINS, Michael: *A History of London Transport, Vol. 1*, London 1963, p. 7.
[27] IBID., p. 241 ff.; FRÖMEL, Susanne: „Moderne Zeiten", in: *Geo Epoche. Das Magazin für Geschichte 18 (London. Geschichte einer Weltstadt, 1558-1945)*, Hamburg 2005, p. 127; see chapter 6.1.2.
[28] KLÜVER, Reymer: „Der Baumeister der Metropole", in: *Geo Epoche. Das Magazin für Geschichte 18 (London. Geschichte einer Weltstadt, 1558-1945)*, Hamburg 2005, p. 110ff.
[29] WIKIPEDIA: *History of London*.

London nor by the authorities.[30] From today's point of view, however, it is hardly understandable why such reasonable plans did not fit in people's minds those days.

Nonetheless, many places which are still known in the 21st century were built in the period of around fifty years after the Great Fire, such as Grosvenor Square, Hanover Square, Berkeley Square. Other famous sites like Leicester Square, St. James's Square, and King Square had already been built in the late 1670's up to the early 1680's.[31] A prominent exception might be Trafalgar Square, which was under construction only during the 1830's.[32]

3.2.2   Improvements under King George IV

The victory over the French fleet at Trafalgar and the decline of Napoleon ten years later made the British Empire remain unchallenged at sea, and so was its position as predominant power, doubtlessly at least in Europe.[33] King George IV had the feeling of being great and unbeatable and the constant competition with France made him measure his architect's results with the shining example of Paris.[34]

The task of building a new boulevard (Regent Street) through the labyrinth of tiny lanes was given to John Nash, the King's favoured architect. At the end of the new street he was supposed to design a park for the King (Regent's Park), which the latter could reach from his residence via Regent Street. But compared to other glamorous avenues, Nash's Regent Street did not describe a straight line when it was completed. Though it looked gorgeous and is now seen as the most important project in London's early metropolitan planning, many compromises had to be accepted. Parliament approved the planning and the size of funds in general but the building of houses was carried out by private people. Every client was allowed to engage his own architect but, fortunately, the supervision of those individual projects was granted to Nash, which allowed him to co-ordinate the appearance of Regent Street to some extent.[35]

At the same time, John Nash was building numerous houses and residences (Buckingham Palace is the most famous example), and after he had given London a link road from the

---

[30] See chapter 2.3.

[31] GEORGIAN LONDON STREET AND BUSINESS INDEX: *Squares.*

[32] Trafalgar Square was built as a tribute to the won battle of Trafalgar in 1805 (GEORGIAN LONDON STREET AND BUSINESS INDEX: *Squares*).

[33] LENZE, Franz: „Die Mutter des Imperiums", in: *Geo Epoche. Das Magazin für Geschichte 18 (London. Geschichte einer Weltstadt, 1558-1945)*, Hamburg 2005, p. 144.

[34] KLÜVER, Reymer: „Der Baumeister der Metropole", in: *Geo Epoche. Das Magazin für Geschichte 18 (London. Geschichte einer Weltstadt, 1558-1945)*, Hamburg 2005, p. 115.

[35] IBID., p. 115ff.

east to the west with Regent Street, he was able to do it likewise from the north to the south.[36] When King George IV died in 1830, Nash was quickly replaced because he was losing his reputation due to several discrepancies in managing the budget.[37]

4   A Century in Which Transportation Approached Undreamt Dimensions

After having seen the development of London's town and the problematic nature of city planning and decent traffic flow yet before the end of the 18th century, the circumstances of the first half of the 19th century will be focused on in this chapter. Concerning the traffic, not many improvements could be made during 18th century. The construction of larger streets had been a step into the right direction and was urgently needed, but the congestions could not have been eased only because of these measures.

What differentiated the 19th century from all epochs before was the flood of new technical inventions which set off. From the railway at the beginning to the electricity at the end, everything appeared within this period. The stage for far reaching changes was set and the realisation of an underground railway was no longer in the distant future. Not at least, the massive increase of population which had never been seen before in such dimensions challenged and urged London's officials.

4.1   Extensions of Urban Public Transportation

4.1.1   Non-Standardised Departments

The bounds which were set by politics to beginning of the 19th century were everything but comfortable with regard to urban development. Inside the area of London, around three hundred municipalities and local authorities were taking decisions on their former village sites, which had earlier amalgamated to a cosmopolitan city and no mayor was elected to represent the capital. Additionally, the national Parliament intervened directly into the city's businesses. It took decisions like building new main streets and, spectacularly, in 1829, the Home Secretary established a uniformed police authority for Greater London, (still today known as) *The Metropolitan Police*. But in general, the growth of traffic and the way the city

---

[36] KLÜVER, Reymer: „Der Baumeister der Metropole", in: *Geo Epoche. Das Magazin für Geschichte 18 (London. Geschichte einer Weltstadt, 1558-1945)*, Hamburg 2005, p. 118f.
[37] IBID.; MEYER, Joseph (ed.): *Meyers grosses Universallexikon, Vol. 5*, Mannheim/Vienna/Zurich 1982, p. 504; BRITANNIA: *History of London*.

was developing had been left to their own fate.[38] The number of inhabitants had reached the edge of one million by then and was increasing day after day.[39]

4.1.2 From Hackney Carriages to the Omnibus

Having already dealt with the 17th century hackney carriages in chapter 3.1.2, the issue of horse drawn coaches had not lost any of its topicality in the early 19th century. The main reason might have been the lack of opportunity to decide between different kinds of means of transportation. Accordingly, carriages were the only alternative to walking or horse riding. River boat services had limited access to individual destinations (although the river Thames is considered a sort of highway of those times)[40] and were probably not remarkably faster, depending on the passengers' route.

Before 1800, the expansion of London's city centre took mainly place along the river Thames and not many people lived far from it.[41] This changed around 1800 when outlying villages grew rapidly and the roads linking them to the centre in the south quickly became important. Many new homes were built along these streets and empty spaces between London and its neighbouring countryside had been filled up all of a sudden.[42]

Additionally to the existing long-stage coaches which brought travellers from farther destinations to the city, a new possibility of travelling appeared; short-stage coaches picked up residents form their homes and gave them a lift to their city destination. The tickets were sold in advance in one of the offices next to the route, but a lot of passengers who were not familiar with the regulations turned up without a tickets. Arguments about the fees for individual journeys stretched the duration of travelling to an unbearable degree.[43] A French visitor reported that he "never saw anything so ill managed [...] [and they] stopped more than twenty times on the road"[44] until he reached Hyde Park Corner after a journey of two hours starting from Richmond which is not more than a dozen miles away.[45] This all seemed to be rather uncomfortable and inefficient, and most strikingly, this was only about short-distance travelling.

---

[38] FRÖMEL, Susanne: „Moderne Zeiten", in: *Geo Epoche. Das Magazin für Geschichte 18 (London. Geschichte einer Weltstadt, 1558-1945)*, Hamburg 2005, p. 127ff.
[39] WIKIPEDIA: *History of London.*
[40] BARKER, T.C./ROBBINS, Michael: *A History of London Transport, Vol. 1*, London 1963, p. 1.
[41] IBID.
[42] IBID., p. 2ff.
[43] IBID., p. 4ff.
[44] IBID., p. 4.
[45] IBID.

These stage coach styled vehicles were in direct competition to the hackney carriages and had, in comparison, the advantage of taking more than double the number of passengers. Although different kinds of hackney carriages had been established, they were never able to carry more than a maximum of three people. Hence, their long lasting monopoly came under pressure, whereas short-stage coaches had detailed advice on where to pick up and drop off passengers, only to prevent the hackneys from bad businesses.[46]

In the late 1820's, a businessman called George Shillibeer was working for a coach builder and stable keeper in Paris. He was an eyewitness of a successfully introduced vehicle, drawn by more than one horse and having seats for up to twenty people – the omnibus. Generally, it resembled the earlier fashionable long-stage coach; in fact, it was not more than a large box on four wheels. Starting his own business in London around 1830, Shillibeer began to run his first route from Paddington to the outskirts and his self-built omnibuses were pulled by three instead of two horses. Within a short time, he was able to enlarge his services and providing more comfortable, larger, and, not least, cheaper omnibuses.[47]

To their disappointment, the Hackney Coach Commission had been abolished by Parliament almost the same time as omnibuses appeared in London and only four years later the limitation of hackney carriages were eased. Quickly, other operators were running omnibus services and accelerated the downfall of hackney coaches.[48]

4.1.3 The First Railways

Some decades had passed by when Scottish engineer James Watt patented his first steam engine in 1769.[49] The idea of using steam power for mobility purposes had probably been kept in mind since then, and before the first locomotive was built, some road-carriages were motorised with steam engines. Their success, however, was very small and vehicles often broke down because of bad road conditions and immature technology.[50] Not to forget the locomotion on the river Thames, where upgraded boats with steam engines already plied routes from 1815 and functioned well as opposed to the steam driven coaches.[51]

On 8 February 1836, *The London & Greenwich Railway Company* opened London's first line, which ran from Deptford to Spa Road only to be extended to London Bridge the

---

[46] BARKER, T.C./ROBBINS, Michael: *A History of London Transport, Vol. 1*, London 1963, p. 6ff.
[47] IBID., p. 14ff.
[48] IBID.
[49] MEYER, Joseph (ed.): *Meyers grosses Universallexikon, Vol. 3*, Mannheim/Vienna/Zurich 1982, p. 414; IBID., *Vol. 15*, p. 286.
[50] BARKER, T.C./ROBBINS, Michael: *A History of London Transport, Vol. 1*, London 1963, p. 43ff.
[51] IBID., p. 40ff.

same year. Their trains worked faultlessly and showed the suitability of railways in short-distance operations. The railway network expanded rapidly and within fewer than two decades, it had reached a considerable size.[52]

During the 1840's, several railway companies were founded and it suddenly became necessary to issue rules in order to control the latest mania of building railway tracks everywhere. *The Royal Commission on Metropolitan Termini* was set up as a controlling body and it prohibited, according to the Government's opinion, the construction of tracks or stations inside a certain area north of Thames. Stations like London Bridge or Fenchurch Street consequently gained importance when new lines shared their favourable location and directed their tracks onto existing ones near them.[53] One of the farthest reaching consequences is the still lasting fact that every railway track leading to a station built these days, ends in a cul-de-sac.[54] This meant that the city centre remained constantly without rail access up to the middle of the century whilst the number of citizens doubled to a figure of two millions in only fifty years.[55] The only public means of locomotion inside the very centre were the same as mentioned above and the comfort of travelling (not to mention the velocity) did not improve at all.[56]

5   The Origins of London's Underground Railway

After the British people had the opportunity of travelling to London by train, the burning question was how the people who inhabited the very centre of London could travel more comfortably, faster, and cheaper. Adding all the factors shown above that were relevant for the cities of London and Westminster, the lack of open space which might have been used for traffic had then been present for more than two hundred years.[57] The degree of difficulty was increased by the prohibition of building anything in the central area which was favouring railway access.[58] What else remained than digging deep underground, trying almost desperately to solve the long lasting traffic difficulties?

---

[52] BARKER, T.C./ROBBINS, Michael: *A History of London Transport, Vol. 1*, London 1963, p. 44ff.; see illustration 5.
[53] IBID., p. 50ff.; see illustration 5.
[54] See illustrations 3, 5 (red markings show stations with dead ends) and 6.
[55] WIKIPEDIA: *History of London*.
[56] See chapter 4.1.2.
[57] See chapter 3.1.
[58] See chapter 4.1.3.

5.1 How to Bring Passengers Closer to the City Centre

5.1.1 Preparing the Underground

Every single railway company followed its own purposes and for London, this was mainly to bring their passengers as close as possible to their individual destinations in the city centre. On the one hand, a solution might have been the extension of railway lines and the movement of stations closer to the city centre to provide a better service to passengers. The aim was to bring the train stations within walking distance from any point of the city centre, while on the other hand, plans were made by certain companies to penetrate deeper into the centre via underground lines.[59]

The intention of building new termini at the very heart of London did not follow the recommendation of the Royal Commission on Metropolitan Termini and was therefore, politically and practically, not simple to track.[60] It had been the focus on a solution below ground to which involved people paid more attention and that eventually was more successful. Before the 1840's and their so-called railway mania, plans of digging tunnels underneath the town had already been considered. Robert Stephenson, for instance, considered an extension of a railway line which should have run underneath Gower Street. While engineers were used to constructing subways in open space or areas with only few buildings, it was something completely different to build a railway track just below expensive property. The law, however, obliged the constructor to purchase buildings outright even if only a part of them had to be undermined. Therefore, it was desirable to involve as few buildings as possible and to direct the line under public streets and open country. This and the fear of high compensations in case of damage deterred Stephenson from realising his plans.[61]

Other schemes led to nothing as well, but awakened the interest of Charles Pearson and John H. Stevens. Both were city officials and worked out a railway programme as they realised that an underground railway could profitably help to improve the Fleet Valley according to plans which the (official) city favoured. Pearson wrote a brochure in 1845 in which he commended the advantages of a railway running below ground down the Fleet Valley to Farringdon Street which would be "as lofty, light and dry, as airy and cheerful as the West End arcades."[62] Being unsuccessful with their scheme, Pearson and Stevens had a second chance

---

[59] BARKER, T.C./ROBBINS, Michael: *A History of London Transport, Vol. 1*, London 1963, p. 99.
[60] See chapter 4.1.3.
[61] BARKER, T.C./ROBBINS, Michael: *A History of London Transport, Vol. 1*, London 1963, p. 100ff.
[62] IBID., p. 102; FRÖMEL, Susanne: „Moderne Zeiten", in: *Geo Epoche. Das Magazin für Geschichte 18 (London. Geschichte einer Weltstadt, 1558-1945)*, Hamburg 2005, p. 127.

to re-launch it in 1851 when *The City Corporation* was obliged to help out *The Clerkenwell Improvement Commission* (founded as supporting element to work out further plans according to the official ones) financially. Their voice now weighed more and *The Common Council* formed a committee (*City Terminus Company*) to study Pearson's *Railway Terminus and City Improvement Plan*.[63]

5.1.2   The Metropolitan Railway

Shortly after having prepared a parliamentary bill, the City Terminus Company had to compete with a company called *The Bayswater, Paddington and Holborn Bridge Railway*. They intended to construct an underground line from Paddington to King's Cross and their programme was less than half as expensive as Pearson's. The new line should run below the already existing New Road (today's Euston Road)[64] and different to Pearson's scheme, no expensive property had to be bought and knocked down. Pearson stood without any chance when both suggestions were presented to the Parliament and the well promoted plan of William Malins, the head of the Bayswater Railway Company and key mover of their scheme, came through in a single day. After this success, their line was renamed *The North Metropolitan*.[65]

Although Pearson had been unlucky with his intention, the directors of the North Metropolitan took it up again and after certain changes they found a way to reuse it in a more profitable way. The origin to this step had been their principal interest in short-distance travelling, whereas the matter of providing access to the city centre for the main line companies was only of partial importance. At that point of time, the idea of a large central rail terminus had definitely been dropped and the North Metropolitan changed its name, once more, now into *The Metropolitan Railway*.[66]

5.2   Launching the Underground

5.2.1   Last Steps before Construction Work

As mentioned above, the multitude of authorities inside London had often had a retarding effect on larger political projects concerning more than one borough.[67] Fortunately, in

---

[63] BARKER, T.C./ROBBINS, Michael: *A History of London Transport, Vol. 1*, London 1963, p. 101ff.
[64] FRÖMEL, Susanne: „Moderne Zeiten", in: *Geo Epoche. Das Magazin für Geschichte 18 (London. Geschichte einer Weltstadt, 1558-1945)*, Hamburg 2005, p. 131.
[65] BARKER, T.C./ROBBINS, Michael: *A History of London Transport, Vol. 1*, London 1963, p. 103ff.
[66] IBID., p. 107ff.
[67] See chapter 4.1.1.

1855, *The Metropolitan Board of Works* had been founded to take over the whole responsibility for two pressing issues, the construction of decent sewers and the coordination of road building. It was the first time in London's history that a single authority handled affairs concerning the entire city.[68]

The progress of the first railway line running below surface still depended on two parties of contrary opinions, the City Corporation and the Metropolitan Railway. Questions concerning the building costs were difficult to answer and just when the war between Britain and Russia broke out in 1856, bank rates rose quickly. Pearson reappeared on the scene in 1857 to push the scheme forward and helped together with the Corporation to find a consensus. His efforts led to a large public meeting in December 1858 under the leadership of the Lord Mayor and after lengthy negotiations both sides signed an agreement.[69]

5.2.2 *"Cut and Cover" and How to Operate Trains*

In spring 1860, construction workers began to tear up New Road in St. Pancras. Little time passed until a ditch was dug that had the width of the road. The houses on both sides as well as the edges of the ditch had to be supported extensively.[70] This method was called *Cut and Cover* and was simple as opening the street, fitting two railway tracks to the ground, covering it with a roof made of bricks and re-establishing the road surface. Consequently, the track level was only five to ten meters underneath ground level.[71] Unfortunately, not every part of the new line ran exactly along the same route as the roads did and many buildings had to cease to exist in favour of the ambitious project. Until the Metropolitan had completed its underground line, around 12,000 people were made to move somewhere else.[72]

With respect to the difference of height between street and underground level, it probably was of great importance that trains were not moving too deep below the surface; the locomotives were all operating with steam power. It might have been essential to have ventilation shafts as short as ever possible, thus guaranteeing a well-functioning exchange of air. Exactly the same issue came up in Parliament when Malins had to answer how he felt about making the trains move.[73] An option without emissions was a cable hauled railway which had

---

[68] FRÖMEL, Susanne: „Moderne Zeiten", in: *Geo Epoche. Das Magazin für Geschichte 18 (London. Geschichte einer Weltstadt, 1558-1945)*, Hamburg 2005, p. 131.

[69] BARKER, T.C./ROBBINS, Michael: *A History of London Transport, Vol. 1*, London 1963, p. 110ff.

[70] FRÖMEL, Susanne: „Moderne Zeiten", in: *Geo Epoche. Das Magazin für Geschichte 18 (London. Geschichte einer Weltstadt, 1558-1945)*, Hamburg 2005, p. 131.

[71] IBID.; WIKIPEDIA: *London Underground*.

[72] FRÖMEL, Susanne: „Moderne Zeiten", in: *Geo Epoche. Das Magazin für Geschichte 18 (London. Geschichte einer Weltstadt, 1558-1945)*, Hamburg 2005, p. 132.

[73] BARKER, T.C./ROBBINS, Michael: *A History of London Transport, Vol. 1*, London 1963, p. 109.

the advantage of being pulled by an external engine and of protecting train users from heavy smoke. But many disadvantages were obvious, too: The limitation of trains on a certain route, for instance, or the large space needed to contain the cable drums. Further on, it seemed rather difficult to extend an existing line and the total length was given by the capacity of rolling up cable anyway.[74] All in all, this technique was only useful for specific purposes but not for projects such as the intended underground railway where neither final proportions were predictable, nor an end of London's growth was in sight.

What remained was merely the issue of steam driven locomotives and Malins found a way to convince a majority of the Parliament. He suggested "to start with our boiler charged with steam and water of such capacity and of such pressure as will take its journey from end to end and then, [...] raise it up again to its original pressure."[75] This consideration promised a weaker production of smoke and succeeded over the critics who had not had such an optimistic view of this affair.[76]

5.2.3 Building Site Accidents and Delays

A timetable which planned the completion of the *Metropolitan Line* between Paddington and Farringdon Street within twenty-one months had been set in advance.[77] At the same time the Fleet sewer was und construction and in June 1862 it burst and flooded the building site near King's Cross. Miraculously, there were no casualties but the progression of work was thrown back for months.[78] The appointment fell behind schedule and the line could not open before the end of 1862.[79] No more major accidents or time delays are recorded and therefore no fatally injured workers had to be lamented. This seems rather remarkable as construction work during the 19th century had often been very dangerous and the protection of workers had been strongly neglected.

5.3 Opening and Operation of the Underground

5.3.1 The World's First Underground Railway

On 3 January 1863, the Metropolitan Railway passed the final inspection of its first underground line. The following week had to be spent on instruction and training of the future

---

[74] BARKER, T.C./ROBBINS, Michael: *A History of London Transport, Vol. 1*, London 1963, p. 48ff.
[75] IBID., p. 109.
[76] IBID., p. 109ff.
[77] IBID., p. 114ff.
[78] IBID., p. 115; FRÖMEL, Susanne: „Moderne Zeiten", in: *Geo Epoche. Das Magazin für Geschichte 18 (London. Geschichte einer Weltstadt, 1558-1945)*, Hamburg 2005, p. 131.
[79] BARKER, T.C./ROBBINS, Michael: *A History of London Transport, Vol. 1*, London 1963, p. 114ff.

staff and on 10 January, the opening ceremony took place.[80] To bring this innovation into service was a unique event to the world and meant the beginning of a new era in transportation history. What was operated from that day on, was a line of 6.5 kilometres (4 miles) length and is still part of today's *Circle Line* and *Hammersmith & City Line*. Also, it partially belongs to the present (and initially name-giving) Metropolitan Line.[81]

5.3.2 The Inner Circuit

Following the success of the Metropolitan Line, the eagerness to construct new surface railway lines reached a second peak in 1863.[82] As during the 1840's, Parliament influenced the railway development and recommended an "inner circle" underground as to link the new and well frequented main-line termini such as Victoria, Charing Cross or Cannon Street.[83] Caused by rivalries amongst different railway companies, another twenty-one years passed by until the inner circuit was closed to a circle. Six railway companies participated and enabled operating the *Circle Line*, which opened in 1884.[84]

5.3.3 The Tube

Up to the late 1880's, the network of Cut and Cover railways had been extended to a handful of lines. All of the companies involved still operated their locomotives with steam power. Some attempts to dig tunnels at deeper levels and with a technique different to Cut and Cover had been made previously, but were unsuccessful. This was not chiefly because of the tunnelling but the planned cable system was simply unsatisfactory.[85] A reason to push such an effort forward were the construction costs for subsurface lines, which were almost prohibitive as the completion of the Circle Line had demonstrated. But as long as no replacement for steam engines could be found, the issues of air pollution and tunnel ventilation could not be solved.[86]

---

[80] BARKER, T.C./ROBBINS, Michael: *A History of London Transport, Vol. 1*, London 1963, p. 115.
[81] SCHLEIFE, Hans-Werner: *Lexikon, Metros der Welt. Geschichte, Technik, Betrieb*, Stuttgart 1985, p. 173; see illustrations 4 and 6.
[82] BARKER, T.C./ROBBINS, Michael: *A History of London Transport, Vol. 1*, London 1963, p. 138, 148; see chapter 4.1.3.
[83] BARKER, T.C./ROBBINS, Michael: *A History of London Transport, Vol. 1*, London 1963, p. 138; see illustration 3.
[84] BARKER, T.C./ROBBINS, Michael: *A History of London Transport, Vol. 1*, London 1963, p. 225; WIKIPEDIA: *London Underground*; see illustration 6.
[85] BARKER, T.C./ROBBINS, Michael: *A History of London Transport, Vol. 1*, London 1963, p. 300ff.; see chapter 5.2.2.
[86] BARKER, T.C./ROBBINS, Michael: *A History of London Transport, Vol. 1*, London 1963, p. 303; see chapter 5.2.2.

It was in Berlin in 1879, that Werner von Siemens presented the first reliable locomotive powered by electricity.[87] The electrification of railways gave a new impulse to the interest in London's underground railway. Also, the opportunity to go for deeper lines automatically reappeared with the issue of air quality being solved (the dependence on steam power was no longer present.[88] Only a good decade later, in December 1890, *The City & South London Railway* started its service on the world's first electric deep level line, which today is part of the *Northern Line*.[89] It was the Prince of Wales (who later became King Edward VII) who appeared in person to put the line into operation and to let the current flow into the cables by turning a key.[90] While tunnelling techniques had been enhanced, the method of Cut and Cover (and therefore the construction of sub-surface lines) was no longer in use as it did not help to connect the quarters south of the river Thames with the city centre.[91] Having to tunnel under a river again signified a notable step in transportation improvements.[92]

London's subsoil consists mainly of clay and is therefore suitable for tunnelling. This helped the constructors to drive a kind of huge milling cutter (called tunnelling shield) into the clay and form a tube-shaped tunnel. At a second stage, the walls were covered with cast iron rings and the completion reinforced with cement.[93] The original shape was not changed by the completion of the tunnel and was name giving to the underground railway. The nickname *Tube* became established when the third deep level line began to run a service in 1900. No matter how long a journey between Shepherd's Bush and Bank took, the fare remained two Pence and the *Central Line* was therefore called *Two Penny Tube*.[94]

---

[87] SCHLEIFE, Hans-Werner: *Lexikon, Metros der Welt. Geschichte, Technik, Betrieb*, Stuttgart 1985, p. 64; MEYER, Joseph (ed.): *Meyers grosses Universallexikon, Vol. 13.*, Mannheim/Vienna/Zurich 1982, p. 38.

[88] BARKER, T.C./ROBBINS, Michael: *A History of London Transport, Vol. 1*, London 1963, p. 303; see chapter 5.2.2.

[89] HAVERS, Harold C.P.: *Die Untergrundbahnen der Welt*, Munich 1966, p. 138; see illustration 6.

[90] BARKER, T.C./ROBBINS, Michael: *A History of London Transport, Vol. 1*, London 1963, p. 310; FRÖMEL, Susanne: „Moderne Zeiten", in: *Geo Epoche. Das Magazin für Geschichte 18 (London. Geschichte einer Weltstadt, 1558-1945)*, Hamburg 2005, p. 136.

[91] WIKIPEDIA: *London Underground*; BARKER, T.C./ROBBINS, Michael: *A History of London Transport, Vol. 1*, London 1963, p. 300ff.

[92] Of course, a traditional tunnelling technique enabled the construction of tunnels in hills and mountains before the building of the City & South London Line (e.g. 728 yards of the Metropolitan Line had been tunnelled where Cut and Cover was inappropriate). In 1843, a pedestrian tunnel had already been built underneath the river Thames. Nonetheless, it was not until 1890 that – thanks to the new technique – it became possible to tunnel under a river without having to start next to the bank (SCHLEIFE, Hans-Werner: *Lexikon, Metros der Welt. Geschichte, Technik, Betrieb*, Stuttgart 1985, p. 173; BARKER, T.C./ROBBINS, Michael: *A History of London Transport, Vol. 1*, London 1963, p. 114).

[93] BARKER, T.C./ROBBINS, Michael: *A History of London Transport, Vol. 1*, London 1963, p. 300ff.

[94] HAVERS, Harold C.P.: *Die Untergrundbahnen der Welt*, Munich 1966, p. 139; see illustration 6.

6 Fares and Affordability of Public Transport to Middle and Lower Social Classes

Two Pence for a trip on an underground train seems affordable to everyone from the point of view of more than a century after the establishment of the Two Penny Tube. But this was not the case and because the field of expenses has not been researched so far, this chapter examines the affordability of the underground system to the public. Especially social classes without financial reserves like the class of labourers are of interest as price reductions or rising prices changed their habits rapidly. This part of the population was the most sensitive in reaction to fare changes and it was also the vast social majority so that operators of public transport companies immediately felt their reactions to slight price modifications.

6.1 The First Commuters and Their Settlements in the Outskirts

6.1.1 The Idea of Commuting

Returning to Charles Pearson, who is already familiar to us, it is important to show the second part of his idea of an underground traffic network.[95] When Pearson appeared on the scene in the mid-1840's, he was not only keen on commending an efficient means of underground transport which he wished to be "as lofty, light and dry [...] as the West End arcades"[96], but he also had in mind to provide the Londoners an opportunity to live in healthier areas than the city centre.[97] He wanted them to live in green and clean surroundings and to commute between the new home and the workplace. Obviously, he was frankly interested in an enhancement of living conditions of the less-wealthy had been condemned to living under bad circumstances until then. That is why he is thought to be the intellectual father of the suburbs, the settlements situated at the edge of the city which grew rapidly from the introduction of the railway to the present time.[98] Unfortunately, Pearson missed the opening of the Metropolitan Line because he died just four months earlier but nevertheless, he was able to see that construction work was on its right way.[99]

---

[95] FRÖMEL, Susanne: „Moderne Zeiten", in: *Geo Epoche. Das Magazin für Geschichte 18 (London. Geschichte einer Weltstadt, 1558-1945)*, Hamburg 2005, p. 132; see chapter 5.1.1ff.
[96] See chapter 5.1.1.
[97] FRÖMEL, Susanne: „Moderne Zeiten", in: *Geo Epoche. Das Magazin für Geschichte 18 (London. Geschichte einer Weltstadt, 1558-1945)*, Hamburg 2005, p. 132.
[98] BARKER, T.C./ROBBINS, Michael: *A History of London Transport, Vol. 2*, London 1974, p. 4ff; see illustration 7.
[99] BARKER, T.C./ROBBINS, Michael: *A History of London Transport, Vol. 1*, London 1963, p. 100f., 115ff.

6.1.2 Fares and Working Class Trains

At the point of time when the first railway lines offered their service to the public, there was no danger for horse pulled coaches to run bad businesses. It was not only because of the lower fares that buses were still popular; as shown further above, the trains were yet unable to reach the centre and apart from that, the seating capacity of omnibuses could be doubled by increasing the number of seats within eleven years until 1850. While the number of seats and passengers was increasing, the fares were dropping because the costs per mile could be distributed onto more travellers.[100] Another reason might be seen in the fact that a vast majority of people still lived next to their place of work and were therefore able to reach it by road.[101] This changed when the Metropolitan provided centrally situated stations and a first class journey (six pence for any distance between Paddington and Farringdon Street) was much more comfortable (but also more expensive) than sitting in an omnibus. A third class journey (three pence), on the other hand, was often cheaper than buses and many needs could be satisfied this way.[102]

Regardless of the lower prices, many people could not afford public traffic either way. Only when fares had dropped again (e.g. one penny for third class passengers between adjoining stations from August 1865), a growing number of commuters who could have walked started using the Tube for the first time.[103] According to Pearson's Act of 1860, the installation of workmen's trains was an integral part. It happened so in May 1864, when the Metropolitan began to operate third class trains for labourers, usually one at 5.30 a.m. and a second one ten minutes later at a return fare of three pence.[104] Until the end of 1865, up to 2,000 workmen were using those trains on weekdays and in February the following year, the *Chatham Railway* started to provide trains between Victoria and Ludgate Hill for workers as well.[105] In the mornings, a train left each terminus at 4.55 a.m. and carried the same passengers at home at 6.15 p.m. and at 2.15 p.m. on Saturdays for a general fare of two pence for any distance on the route.[106] Of course, on Sundays no such service was provided as these trains were especially appointed to working class people on working days.

---

[100] BARKER, T.C./ROBBINS, Michael: *A History of London Transport, Vol. 1*, London 1963, p. 56ff.; see chapter 4.1.3.
[101] BARKER, T.C./ROBBINS, Michael: *A History of London Transport, Vol. 1*, London 1963, p. 53ff.
[102] IBID., p. 171ff.
[103] IBID., p. 172ff.
[104] IBID., p. 116.
[105] See illustration 6.
[106] BARKER, T.C./ROBBINS, Michael: *A History of London Transport, Vol. 1*, London 1963, p. 173.

Ten years after the first engagement of workmen's trains, nearly two thirds (64 percent) who travelled on the Metropolitan were third class passengers.[107] This is a considerable percentage compared to the remaining third that used first or second class trains. It was therefore an important step to reduce fares in order to ensure mobility to the poorer parts of society.

6.1.3 The Loss of Residents in Central Areas

Before the introduction of the underground railway, London's residents normally lived next to work and were not willing to move to or beyond the city boundaries. But when the economic climate in Britain changed, the growth of suburban areas increased. This was caused by many middle class people who profited from the economic boom and who quickly decided to use parts of their risen income for living at the edge of or outside the city. Between 1851 and 1901, the number of residents in the City of London fell from 128,000 to 27,000; almost eighty percent of the permanent population had moved away from the heart of London within fifty years. In a similar space of time, the day population (commuters) increased from 170,000 in 1866 to 360,000 in 1901; this was more than a doubling in only thirty-five years. Westminster and Holborn, two other centrally situated quarters, experienced a similar trend.[108]

Commuting also gained importance in fields of activities not related to work. While weekly working hours had been reduced in the last quarter of the century, people increasingly followed leisure activities. They had more time to spend with their families and off-peak travelling for pleasure purposes flourished. Previously inhabited facilities were now changed into offices, shops and department stores. This produced new habits and brought people to central and suburban shopping streets by underground railway.[109] At the beginning of the 20th century, the process of depopulation (referred to the central quarter's residents) was nearly completed. The city became the economic heart of the capital and it also became common to sleep and live in the outskirts and work in the centre. London had anticipated an urban development which was to be experienced by many cities all over the world during the 20th century.[110]

---

[107] BARKER, T.C./ROBBINS, Michael: *A History of London Transport, Vol. 1*, London 1963, p. 173.
[108] IBID., p. 198ff.
[109] IBID., p. 198ff.
[110] FRÖMEL, Susanne: „Moderne Zeiten", in: *Geo Epoche. Das Magazin für Geschichte 18 (London. Geschichte einer Weltstadt, 1558-1945)*, Hamburg 2005, p. 136.

7 Mind the Gap – London Underground Today

Before we draw a conclusion and analyse the previous chapters, this chapter contains a brief overview of the 20th century and is then focusing on the situation of London's underground railway today. It is also a retrospective summary and gives an answer to the second issue which I have set at the beginning.[111]

7.1 The Development of the Tube during the 20th Century

7.1.1 New Tube Lines after the City & South London and further Electrifications

Still in 1890, the City & South London Railway showed a tendency towards the electrification of deep level lined.[112] Many plans had been made until then but the financing had always been the core problem. In 1900, however, *The Central London Railway* opened the third Tube line (today part of the *Central Line*)[113] and was internationally supported in doing so.[114] The second one was the *Waterloo & City Line*, which had been put into service only two years before and which had a length of merely 2.4 kilometres (1.5 miles). It was limited by the stations Waterloo and Bank which has not changed until nowadays. This line has no intermediate stations and was only built to link a large main-line station with the City. The Waterloo & City Line was not included in the underground network (*London Transport*)[115] and was operated by the *British Rail* (the later formed national railway association) until 1994.[116] In 1905 und 1906, the first built sub-surface lines, the Metropolitan and *District Railway*, were both electrified.[117]

As for the period before the outbreak of the Second World War, two more Tube lines have to be mentioned; The *Baker* Street & Water*loo* Line (later shortened to *Bakerloo Line*) and the *Piccadilly Line* were both completed in 1906. Additionally, the Hammersmith & City (built in 1864) and the *East London Line* (1869), both sub-surface lines, need to be mentioned to give a coherent image of the state of existing railway companies before the 1940's.[118] All companies constantly extended their lines as London was growing fast and had its most dramatic increase of population during the 19th century (from on million inhabitants in 1800 to

---

[111] See chapter 1.
[112] See chapter 5.3.3.
[113] WIKIPEDIA: *London Underground*.
[114] BARKER, T.C./ROBBINS, Michael: *A History of London Transport, Vol. 2*, London 1974, p. 35ff.
[115] See chapter 7.2.2.
[116] BARKER, T.C./ROBBINS, Michael: *A History of London Transport, Vol. 2*, London 1974, p. 50f.; HAVERS, Harold C.P.: *Die Untergrundbahnen der Welt*, Munich 1966, p. 138f.; WIKIPEDIA: *London Underground*.
[117] HAVERS, Harold C.P.: *Die Untergrundbahnen der Welt*, Munich 1966, p. 138.
[118] WIKIPEDIA: *London Underground*; see chapter 5.3.

six millions 1900) and it continued accordingly in the first third of the 20th century.[119] Instead of reconstructing every single route extension, another event is of more interest.

7.1.2 London's First Transport Board and the Second World War

After decades of competition between different railway companies, a superior authority was founded in 1933. *The London Passenger Transport Board* was formed to standardise the whole network of underground traffic for the first time in history of what became commonly called *The Underground*.[120] A uniformed policy and appearance were the reasons which led to this step and the board was led by *The London County Council* and no longer by private companies.[121] This unification of various firms brought the ability to act in the name of public interest and not according to the plans of company owners.

During the Nazi bombings on London in 1940, many citizens were using deep-level Tube stations for shelter. They gave them a safe place to stay while the (mainly) nocturnal air raids took place above.[122] Certainly, an issue concerning the future of the nation worried more in those days than those issues concerning the Tube and not much happened to the latter's improvement until the end of war.

7.1.3 The Post-War Period

When war was over, the focus could be reset on civil issues. This happened in early 1948, when London Transport, an organisation which was under the leadership of *The Ministry of Transport*, removed the London Passenger Transport Board. The main responsibility of London Transport was to organise a range of public transportation according to the previously defined transport policy. Furthermore, the network of Tube lines which was already of a considerable size had to be completed with additional routes.[123] To the ten existing lines, another two were added; the *Victoria Line* in 1969 and the *Jubilee Line* ten years later.[124]

Of all line extensions, the 1977 extension of the Piccadilly Line is the most remarkable; it connected London Heathrow Airport with the city centre. Still today, it is the only airport (out of five) which is directly connected by Underground.[125] In the 1970's, officials made another interesting proposal, namely to build a second orbital line through outer London bor-

---

[119] WIKIPEDIA: *History of London*.
[120] BARKER, T.C./ROBBINS, Michael: *A History of London Transport, Vol. 2*, London 1974, p. 276ff.
[121] IBID., p. 270ff.; see chapters 4.1.1 and 4.1.3.
[122] OTTO, Frank: „Tage der Bedrängnis", in: *Geo Epoche. Das Magazin für Geschichte 18 (London. Geschichte einer Weltstadt, 1558-1945)*, Hamburg 2005, p. 162ff.
[123] HAVERS, Harold C.P.: *Die Untergrundbahnen der Welt*, Munich 1966, p. 174.
[124] WIKIPEDIA: *London Underground*.
[125] IBID.; see illustration 6.

oughs. But it never came to be realised as the investment needed seemed too high compared to benefits expected.[126]

7.2 Entry into a new Millennium and Changing Challenges for Public Transport

7.2.1 Status and Importance of Public Transport

By the end of the 20th century, many circumstances for public traffic had changed compared to pioneer days. Most significant is the ownership of private cars which has become more and more common after the war.[127] Before the invention of combustion engines in the late 1800's, private vehicles (e.g. horse pulled coaches) had never been serious competitors for public transport because hardly anyone could afford them and they did not provide higher speed or similar advantages.[128] Walking was the only affordable possibility of movement besides to public transportation.[129]

From the end of the 1940's, the number of registered private cars in the United Kingdom rose more than one thousand percent within thirty years from 1.4 to 14.4 million.[130] With its high impact on cities, private traffic became the most urgent item in urban politics. The decline in use of public transport was the result of the increased personal mobility and the decrease of fare revenues led the operators into financial troubles.[131] At the same time, maintenance and the exchange of old rolling stock drove costs higher and higher and as many other modern mass traffic companies, London Transport had to claim for subsidies.[132]

The Tube lost its original significance of providing services to the whole city population by the time individual traffic became motorised and affordable. Public transportation became a sort of social service rather than a means of transport for everyone.[133] But the use and maintenance of London Underground is undeniable even though more daily journeys are taken by car than by Tube. Today, people set out on a journey throughout Greater London approximately thirty million times every day. Whereas more than a third (or eleven million journeys) of these journeys are taken by car or motorcycle, only ten percent (or three million journeys) are taken by Tube (the total amount of rail travelling is 15 percent or 4.5 million journeys).

---

[126] COLLINS, Michael F./PHAROAH, Timothy M.: *Transport Organisation in a Great City: The Case of London*, London 1974, p. 217ff.
[127] PACIONE, Michael: *Urban Problems: An Applied Urban Analysis*, London/New York 1990, p. 160.
[128] See chapter 3.1.1 and 3.1.2.
[129] See chapter 4.1.2.
[130] PACIONE, Michael: *Urban Problems: An Applied Urban Analysis*, London/New York 1990, p. 160.
[131] IBID., p. 168ff.
[132] PACIONE, Michael: *Urban Problems: An Applied Urban Analysis*, London/New York 1990, p. 168ff.; WIKIPEDIA: *London Underground*.
[133] PACIONE, Michael: *Urban Problems: An Applied Urban Analysis*, London/New York 1990, p. 169.

Still, three million passengers a day do justify the operation of London Underground. The responsibility for operation is now taken by *Transport for London (TfL)*, an organisation which was created in the year 2000 as a new integrated body for all transport systems of the city.[134]

7.2.2 Incidents of 7 July 2005 and Security Issues

In the mid-morning of 7 July 2005, a series of bomb blasts shook the City of London and its underground railway system just when commuter traffic drew to a close. Shortly later, it turned out to be an attack of terrorists suspected to be in relation with the Middle East terrorist network al-Qaeda. Within less than an hour, they blew up Underground railway carriages at three different sites and they also ripped a double-decker bus into shreds. Around fifty people were killed and seven hundred injured by the end of that day.[135]

Neither the United Kingdom nor London Underground has ever seen such a disaster. Even *Irish Republican Army (IRA)* bombings had not been as well-coordinated and destructive as the happenings of "Black Thursday". The very next day, newspapers were filled with articles about future security measures and how the horrific attacks could have been avoided. Most politicians reacted calmer than their colleagues did after the New York disaster in September 2001. Nonetheless, many people condemned the incidents resolutely but extreme proposals to solve the terrorist problem remained a peripheral phenomenon.[136] One example of an unrealistic and unaffordable proposal I heard of in those days was the conversion of all Tube stations to enable an airport style check-in of passengers. It is unimaginable how long it would take a commuter to reach his or her workplace not to forget the queues in front of stations blocking streets and traffic far away from it. Three million customers are too many to handle this way and the likely economic damage obviously deterred people as no similar suggestions had been made after a short time.

7.2.3 Future Prospects

Currently, the Tube has to be sufficient for thousands of working people and tourists travelling through Britain's capital. To ensure this capacity, several measures had to be taken such as the hiring of part time employees during peak hours or some long-term financing to exchange or refurbish old material. The government intended to provide £16 billion until

---

[134] TRANSPORT FOR LONDON (TfL): *Description*.
[135] BRITISH BROADCASTING CORPORATION (BBC): *London Attacks*; THE TIMES, INTERNATIONAL EDITION: *Friday, 8 July 2005*.
[136] THE TIMES, INTERNATIONAL EDITION: *Friday, 8 July 2005*.

2030 to cut delays and improve not only rolling stock but also stations and their heavily strained parts such as lifts or escalators.[137]

Additionally, further standardisations are urgently needed but are expensive and take a lot of time. Still today, many different types of wagon are in use even though it would be better (and is intended so) to remove them in favour of a single type thus making for less expensive and easier maintenance.[138] The traces of more than 140 years since the opening of the first underground line can be seen clearly as many parts of the Underground do not fit in modern expectations. Technical knowledge, safety standards, purpose and many other factors were not the same when railway pioneers planned the then new public transportation system.[139]

8 Conclusion

After having discussed all relevant items, I sum them up in this chapter. The answer to the introductory question about the reasons of building an underground railway can already be found in chapter 3. It shows clearly how London's traffic situation was still muddled in the 17th century and how it was impossible to improve it. The foundations for the Underground had therefore been laid when London was growing from a village to a rather large city around 1600.[140] When railways were invented, it was already too late to change the circumstances and to turn around the city's development as London *was* already fully developed. Hence, the constructors of the then new transport system were forced by facts which they could not influence and which finally made them dig tunnels below ground.[141] This also gives an answer to why it all happened so early in history compared to other cities: A railway network seemed to be the only opportunity to solve the traffic problems and the motor-car had not been invented yet.[142]

If we have a look at today's Underground network, 45 percent of all lines (mainly central sections) actually run below ground.[143] The remaining percentage consists of line extensions which were built as the suburbs were growing. Obviously, people were aware of the "underground problem" and included some space for rail tracks above ground whilst planning new sections.

---

[137] WIKIPEDIA: *London Underground.*
[138] IBID.
[139] See chapter 5.2.
[140] See chapter 2.2.
[141] See chapter 5.1.
[142] See chapter 7.2.
[143] WIKIPEDIA: *London Underground.*

In my opinion, the Tube clearly solved mid-19th century traffic problems but simultaneously the city grew at such a speed as a result of the Underground that new difficulties appeared before older ones had been solved. Nevertheless, still at the beginning of the 21st century, travelling by Tube is an intelligent and suitable form of mobility inside London. As shown in chapter 7, many modifications have to be made to satisfy modern society but living without the (old and worn) Tube is unimaginable for almost every Londoner.

9   Illustrations

1   Street Scene on Petticoat Lane, End of the 19th Century

2   Volume of Traffic outside the Royal Exchange, 1896

3   Paddington Station, 1862

4   Gower Street Station, 1873 (renamed Euston Square in 1909)[144]

---

[144] UNDERGROUND HISTORY: *Renamed Stations*.

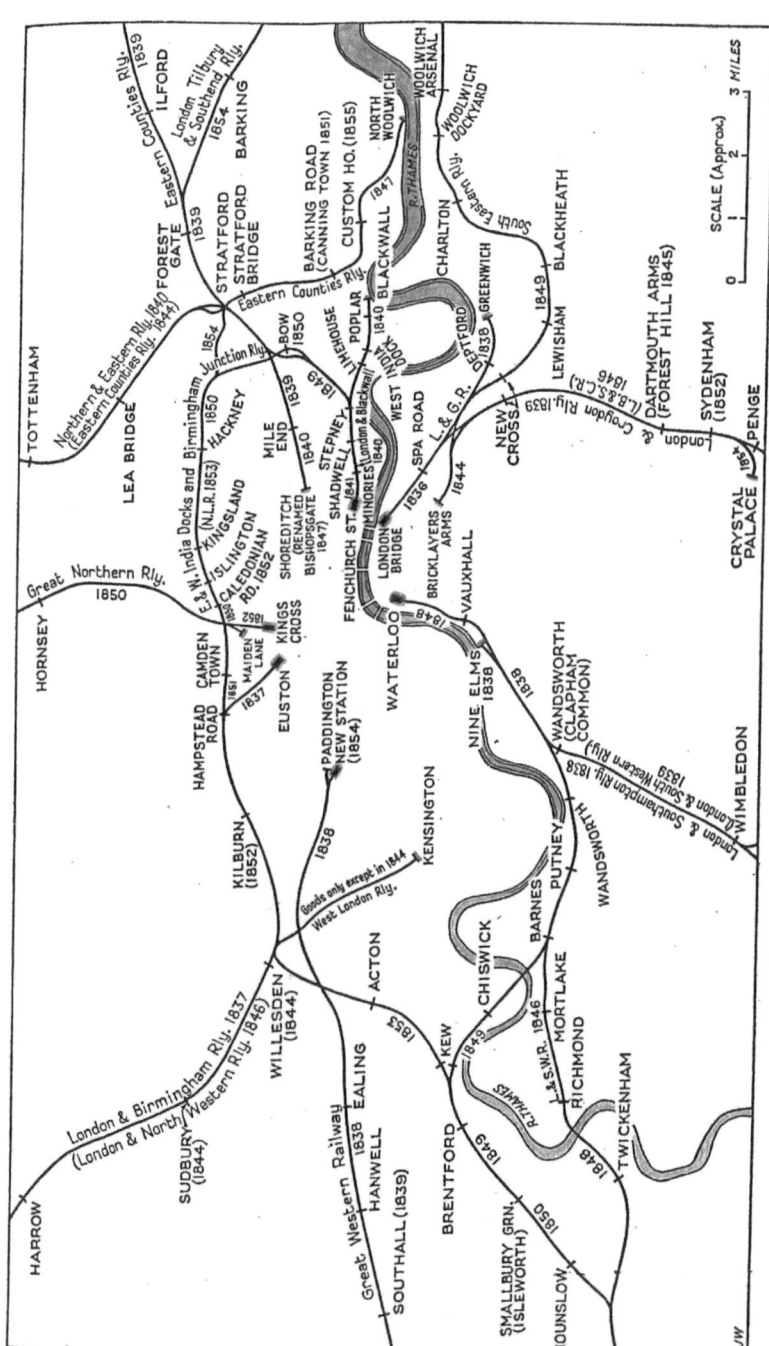

London Railways in 1855

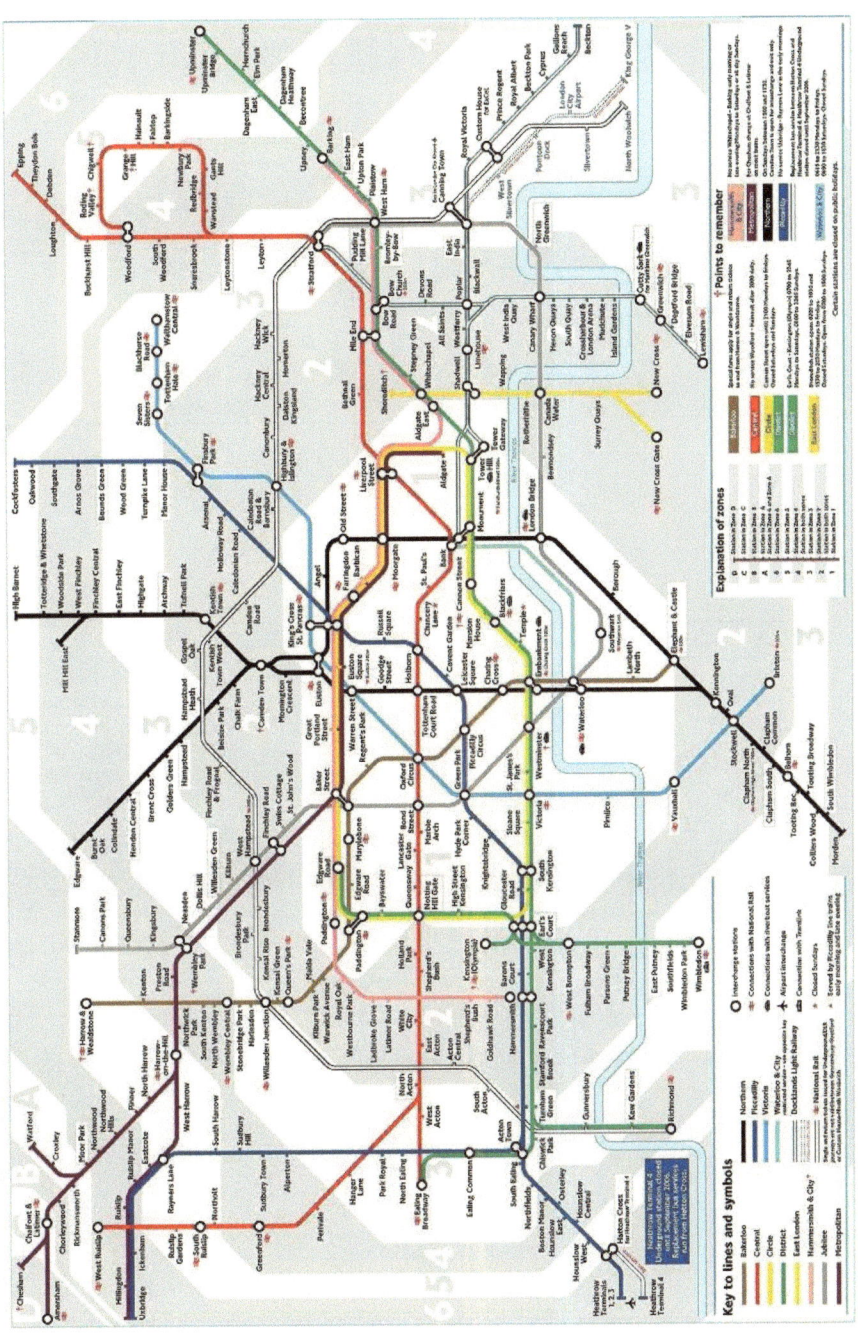

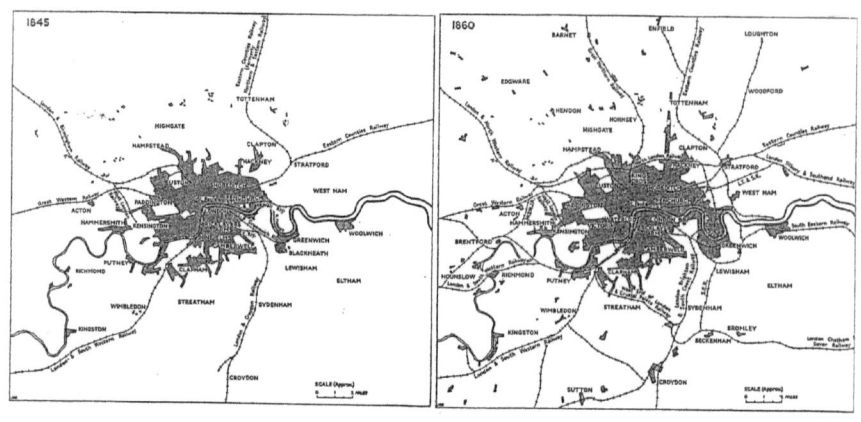

7   The Growth of London and the Increase of Railway Lines, 1845-1900

10 Bibliography

10.1 Printed Sources

MEYER, Joseph (ed.): *Meyers grosses Universallexikon, Vol. 1-15*, Mannheim/Vienna/Zurich 1982: Bibliographisches Institut AG.

THE TIMES, INTERNATIONAL EDITION: *Friday, 8 July 2005.*

10.2 Internet Sources

BRITANNIA: *History of London.*
Online at the Internet: http://www.britannia.com/history/londonhistory/ [accessed on 4 August 2005].

BRITISH BROADCASTING CORPORATION (BBC): *London Attacks.*
Online at the Internet: http://www.bbc.co.uk/1/shared/spl/hi/uk/05/london_blasts/html/ [accessed on 8 July 2005].

BRITISH BROADCASTING CORPORATION (BBC): *Social History (a).*
Online at the Internet: http://www.bbc.co.uk/history/society_culture/society/after_fire _06.shtml [accessed on 28 July 2005].

BRITISH BROADCASTING CORPORATION (BBC): *Social History (b).*
Online at the Internet: http://www.bbc.co.uk/history/society_culture/society/brighter_ lights_04.shtml [accessed on 4 July 2005].

GEORGIAN LONDON STREET AND BUSINESS INDEX: *Squares.*
Online at the Internet: http://www.georgianindex.net/London/squares/L_squares.html [accessed on 4 August 2005].

THE OFFICIAL WEBSITE FOR LONDON: *City Guide.*
Online at the Internet: http://www.visitlondon.com/city_guide/about_london/history/ [accessed on 4 July 2005].

TRANSPORT FOR LONDON (TFL): *Description.*
Online at the Internet: http://www.londontransport.co.uk/tfl/abt_tfl.asp [accessed on 8 November 2005].

UNDERGROUND HISTORY: *Renamed Stations.*
Online at the Internet: http://www.starfury.demon.co.uk/uground/renames.html [accessed on 28 June 2005].

WIKIPEDIA, THE FREE ENCYCLOPEDIA: *History of London.*

Online at the Internet: http://en.wikipedia.org/wiki/History_of_London [accessed on 24 July 2005].

WIKIPEDIA, THE FREE ENCYCLOPEDIA: *London Underground.*

Online at the Internet: http://en.wikipedia.org/wiki/London_Underground [accessed on 4 August 2005].

10.3 Secondary Literature

ALBIG, Jörg-Uwe: „Das geheime Leben der Kapitale", in: *Geo Epoche. Das Magazin für Geschichte 18 (London. Geschichte einer Weltstadt, 1558-1945)*, Hamburg 2005: Gunner + Jahr AG & CO KG, p. 62-79.

BARKER T.C./ROBBINS, Michael: *A History of London Transport: Passenger Travel and the Development of the Metropolis, Vol. 1*, London 1963: George Allen & Unwin Ltd.

BARKER T.C./ROBBINS, Michael: *A History of London Transport: Passenger Travel and the Development of the Metropolis, Vol. 2*, London 1974: George Allen & Unwin Ltd.

COLLINS, Michael F./PHAROAH, Timothy M.: *Transport Organisation in a Great City: The Case of London*, London 1974: George Allen & Unwin Ltd.

FRÖMEL, Susanne: „Moderne Zeiten", in: *Geo Epoche. Das Magazin für Geschichte 18 (London. Geschichte einer Weltstadt, 1558-1945)*, Hamburg 2005: Gunner + Jahr AG & CO KG, p. 122-136.

HAVERS, Harold C.P.: *Die Untergrundbahnen der Welt*, Munich 1966: Moderne Verlags-Gmbh.

KLÜVER, Reymer: „Der Baumeister der Metropole", in: *Geo Epoche. Das Magazin für Geschichte 18 (London. Geschichte einer Weltstadt, 1558-1945)*, Hamburg 2005: Gunner + Jahr AG & CO KG, p. 108-119.

LENZE, Franz: „Die Mutter des Imperiums", in: *Geo Epoche. Das Magazin für Geschichte 18 (London. Geschichte einer Weltstadt, 1558-1945)*, Hamburg 2005: Gunner + Jahr AG & CO KG, p. 140-153.

LOXTON, Howard: *Railways*, London/New York/Sydney/Toronto 1968: Paul Hamlyn.

MISCHER, Olaf/OTTO, Frank: „London. Stadtgeschichte" (Chronik), in: *Geo Epoche. Das Magazin für Geschichte 18 (London. Geschichte einer Weltstadt, 1558-1945)*, Hamburg 2005: Gunner + Jahr AG & CO KG, p. 170-177.

OTTO, Frank: „Tage der Bedrängnis", in: *Geo Epoche. Das Magazin für Geschichte 18 (London. Geschichte einer Weltstadt, 1558-1945)*, Hamburg 2005: Gunner + Jahr AG & CO KG, p. 160-169.

PACIONE, Michael: *Urban Problems: An Applied Urban Analysis*, London/New York 1990: Routledge.

SCHLEIFE, Hans-Werner: *Lexikon, Metros der Welt. Geschichte, Technik, Betrieb*, Stuttgart 1985: Motorbuch Verlag.

10.4 Index of Illustrations

Ill. 1   *Road Scene on Petticoat Lane, End of the 1800's.*
         WARD FAMILY WEBSITE: 1800s Britain.
         Online at the Internet: http://www.ourwardfamily.com/victorian_london.htm [accessed on 27 June 2005].

Ill. 2   *Traffic Scene outside the Royal Exchange, 1896.*
         THE VICTORIAN DICTIONARY: Transport.
         Online at the Internet: http://www.victorianlondon.org/transport/traffic.gif [accessed on 27 June 2005].

Ill. 3   *Paddington Station, 1862.*
         ROYAL HOLLOWAY, UNIVERSITY OF LONDON: Images.
         Online at the Internet: http://rhbnc.ac.uk/picture-gallery/railway.jpg [accessed on 27 June 2005].

Ill. 4   *Gower Street Station, 1873.*
         THE VICTORIAN DICTIONARY: Transport.
         Online at the Internet: http://victorianlondon.org/transport/gowerst.gif [accessed on 27 June 2005].

Ill. 5   *London Railways in 1855.*
         BARKER, T.C./ROBBINS, Michael: *A History of London Transport, Vol. 1*, London 1963, p. 47.

Ill. 6   *Tube Map.*
         TRANSPORT FOR LONDON: Standard Tube Map.
         Online at the Internet: http://www.tfl.gov.uk/tube/maps/ [accessed on 4 August 2005].

Ill. 7 *The Growth of London and the Increase of Railway Lines, 1845-1900.*
    BARKER, T.C./ROBBINS, Michael: *A History of London Transport, Vol. 1*, London
    1963, p. XXVIIIf.